MARTHA GRAHAM

Founder of Modern Dance
by Gerald Newman
and Eleanor Newman Layfield

A Book Report Biography
FRANKLIN WATTS
A Division of Grolier Publishing
New York / London / Hong Kong / Sydney
Danbury, Connecticut

This book is lovingly dedicated to the memory of Linda Weintraub Hochberg, who shared the same birthday as Martha Graham.

Frontispiece: Martha Graham in her solo from *Death and Entrances*, 1944

Cover illustration by Rob Howard, interpretted from photographs by © Photofest

Photographs ©: AP/Wide World Photos: 2, 73, 85, 107, 108, 112, 117; Archive Photos: 101; Barbara Morgan: 9, 17, 36, 39, 55, 59, 62, 63, 64, 67, 69, 75, 93, 118; Harvard Theatre Collection, The Houghton Library: 43; Photofest: cover, 26, 71, 79, 87; UPI/Corbis-Bettmann: 12, 31, 97, 104, 109, 115.

Visit Franklin Watts on the Internet at:
http://publishing.grolier.com

Library of Congress Cataloging-in-Publication Data

Newman, Gerald.
    Martha Graham / Gerald Newman and Eleanor Newman Layfield.
      p. cm.—(A book report biography)
    Includes bibliographical references and index.
    Summary: A biography of the dancer, choreographer, and teacher who is generally considered to be one of America's greatest pioneers of modern dance.
    ISBN 0-531-11442-2
    1. Graham, Martha—Juvenile literature. 2. Dancers—United States—Biography—Juvenile literature. 3. Choreographers—United States—Biography—Juvenile literature. [1. Graham, Martha. 2. Dancers. 3. Choreographers. 4. Women—Biography.] I. Layfield, Eleanor Newman. II. Title. III. Series.
GV1785.G7N49 1998
792.8'028'092—dc21
[B]   98-20410
                                            CIP
                                            AC

© 1998 by Franklin Watts, a division of Grolier Publishing
All rights reserved. Published simultaneously in Canada
Printed in the United States of America
1 2 3 4 5 6 7 8 9 10 R 07 06 05 04 03 02 01 00 99 98

GROLIER
P U B L I S H I N G

CONTENTS

CHAPTER FIVE
A CULTURAL LEGACY

MARTHA GRAHAM'S IMPACT ON MOVEMENT

In the early twentieth century, the arts were in a state of unrest, and the changes that took place began a cultural revolution. Perhaps it was a revolt against the strictness of the Victorian Age. Perhaps it was caused by the bloodshed of the Spanish-American War (1898) or World War I (1914–1918). Whatever the reason, gifted artists such as Igor Stravinsky reinvented tonality and rhythm in music; T. S. Eliot and e. e. cummings brought greater depth to poetry; Frank Lloyd Wright gave another perspective to architecture; and Pablo Picasso changed our way of looking at art.

But dance, probably the oldest form of art, hardly changed. Classical European ballet had remained much the same since its Renaissance beginnings. True, company managers such as Sergei Diaghilev and choreographers such as

Russia's Michel Fokine brought a modern quality to ballet by creating some dances without plot. Of course, long before written history, Asians, Africans, and Native Americans danced as a religious ritual or to enact folk tales. In the 1900s, Isadora Duncan rebelled against the rigid rules of classical ballet and brought a new freedom to dance. But she was considered a lone innovator rather than the creator of an entire movement. And although Ruth St. Denis and Ted Shawn originated an original and creative style that inspired a whole generation of dancers, it was Martha Graham who brought dance into the twentieth century.

Martha Graham created movement that evolved from the meaning of dance and not from traditional ballet steps. And by breaking old rules, she developed new truths. Graham told her students that dance must portray truth. "You must listen to ancestral footsteps, but you must never look back. You must move ahead, believing movement never lies, searching for truth, letting your body speak, knowing technique prepares your body to speak in dance."

"You must move ahead, believing movement never lies. . . ."

Graham broke the old rules of dance, performing in bare feet and using angular movements.

LEARNING ABOUT TRUTH

When Graham was a child, her father once pointed out that she was not telling the truth. "How did you know?" she asked. "I can tell by the way you are moving," he replied. Though at that point Graham had no idea she would become a dancer, she learned a valuable lesson: the language of the body is always the truth.

Another time, her father, a psychiatrist, had invited a female patient to join the family for dinner. The woman did not communicate with anyone at the table, and when she wasn't fidgeting, she sat doubled over. Later, when Martha asked her father why his patient seemed so odd, he told her that the woman's body was saying that she was ill. Her father believed that our bodies can tell a story even if we do not speak.

Once, while speaking with her father, young Martha told him that the water in her glass was "pure." Dr. Graham put a drop of the water on a slide and viewed it with his microscope. He showed his daughter all the tiny creatures living in what she thought was "pure" water. Then he told her that she must always "look for the truth, whatever the truth may be—good, bad, or unsettling."

"I have never forgotten the vividness of that moment, which presided like a star over my life," Graham later wrote in her autobiography. "In a curious way, this was my first dance lesson—a gesture toward the truth."

Truth for Graham was the ability to create her own style of dance, a movement that would be a unique American art form. Like Stravinsky and Picasso, Martha Graham ignored accepted ideas.

Instead of the artificiality of ballet, she favored angular forms and percussive movements. No longer were dancers expected to balance on their toes or defy gravity with their leaps. Her dancers' feet were bare, flat on the ground, and resting at right angles to the leg. No turning out, and no pointing. And there were no tales of princes, princesses, and sprites. Her characters, when she defined them as such, were common people. She drew from everywhere to present Native Americans, settlers, Greek legends, Asian images, and biblical themes—all revealing "the inner human."

HER WIDE INFLUENCE

Graham's pupils ranged from dancers Anna Sokolow, Erick Hawkins, and Merce Cunningham to actors Katherine Cornell, Bette Davis, Gregory Peck, Madonna, Woody Allen, Kathleen Turner, Tony Randall, and Liza Minnelli. She worked with innovative artists such as Isamu Noguchi and Alexander Calder; designers such as Jean Rosenthal and Halston; composers such as Henry Cowell, Paul Hindemith, Igor Stravinsky, Gian Carlo Menotti, and Aaron Copland; and dancers such as Rudolf Nureyev, Mikhail Baryshnikov, and Dame Margot Fonteyn.

Choreographer Agnes de Mille, her friend of sixty years, stated that though Graham may not

*As her reputation grew, Graham worked
with celebrities, such as singer/dancer
Liza Minnelli and the designer Halston.*

have created a new way of moving, she evolved "a
personal expression that was based on simple
running, walking, and leaping." She gave the
dance world a new vocabulary, a new truth in the
hundreds of dances she created during her long
and distinguished career.

John Martin, then a dance critic for *The New York Times,* summed it up best as far back as 1936. "When the definitive history of the dance comes to be written, it will become evident that no other dancer has yet touched the borders to which Martha Graham has extended the compass of movement. . . . She has proved the body capable of a phenomenal range. . . . In the field of creative, expressional movement she has made an incomparable contribution."

CHAPTER ONE

A DANCER'S BEGINNINGS

In 1894, western Pennsylvania was an important coal-mining area of America. Allegheny, a suburb of Pittsburgh situated where the Allegheny, Monongahela, and Ohio Rivers meet, was a sooty gray example of what coal dust could do to a town. It was a depressing sight. Women and girls wore veils to keep the soot off their faces and gloves to keep their hands clean. One Allegheny street contained an arsenal, another a prison, but most were lined with charming houses and churches. There was even an observatory on a hill northwest of the town.

It was here in Allegheny, on May 11, 1894, that Martha Graham was born, about the same time as British authors Aldous Huxley and J. B. Priestly and American humorist James Thurber. It was the year Kipling wrote *The Jungle Book,* Captain Alfred Dreyfus of the French army was convicted of treason, and Claude Debussy composed "Afternoon of a Faun." Grover Cleveland was serving his second term as president of the United States, Victoria was the queen of England, and Nicholas II became the czar of Russia.

Martha's father, Dr. George Greenfield Graham, born in 1856 of Irish ancestry, was called "Goldie" for the color of his hair. Professionally, he was known as an "alienist," a physician who treated patients with nervous or emotional disorders. Today, he would be called a psychiatrist.

Money was never a problem in the Graham household. The costs of Dr. Graham's college and medical school as well as his practice were paid for by a trust fund set up by his father, the first president of the Bank of Pittsburgh. After graduation from medical school, Dr. Graham practiced in Western Pennsylvania Hospital in Dixmont, a town near Allegheny. But in 1893, the year he married Jane Beers, he resigned his position as senior assistant physician and went into private practice.

Dr. Graham was a gentleman, and during their courtship, he often wrote love letters to Jane Beers. One said: "I am awfully sorry that I cannot go and see you as I intended but please accept the floral offering and love me until Saturday, at least, when I hope to see you. Please write to me if nothing more than one word of love. No one can tell how much I thirst for one sight of your dear face . . . I will wait until then. Kisses, George."

Throughout their marriage, the two were filled with admiration and respect for each other. George was a fun-loving and sometimes even boisterous man. He loved music, and after Martha was born, he often played and sang hymns for her or tunes from Gilbert and Sullivan operettas.

DR. GRAHAM'S DAUGHTER

Martha was definitely her father's daughter. As a child, she liked to walk along Main Street with her head covered by a veil. She enjoyed seeing the world through the sheer netting. When an adult tried to kiss her on the cheek, as grown-ups often did in those days, she scolded them. "My father, Dr. Graham, will not permit anyone to kiss me on the face, but you may kiss my hand." One Sunday morning, while she was sitting on her mother's lap in church, Martha recognized a tune being played as one she often danced to at home when her father played the piano. So Martha, all dressed in white, stood up and began dancing down the church aisle. Mrs. Graham was mortified—no one danced in a Presbyterian church—but Martha enjoyed every minute of it.

When she was about four, Martha was unhappy about having to go on a train trip to visit

Martha was born into a loving family and was often considered her father's favorite, probably because she was strong-willed and opinionated.

relatives. In spite of her protests, her mother refused to let her get off the train. Then, as the conductor came by, Martha shouted, "Man, I'm Dr. Graham's daughter and I want out of here!"

Martha thought nothing of disregarding things her parents told her and often misbehaved. When scolded, she spoke back to her father. She knew it was rude, but she believed her father wanted her to develop her own individuality. Her father never hit her or even raised his voice. "Martha, you disappoint me so," was all he would say, which to Martha was more painful than being punished. But he also once told her, "If you are going to make a scandal, make it big."

Martha was Dr. Graham's favorite child, probably because this glib, impudent, strong-willed daughter came closest to being the son he always wanted. He even taught her how to bet on horses.

THE GRAHAM HOUSEHOLD

At twenty-two, Martha's mother was fifteen years younger than Dr. Graham and weighed all of 98 pounds (44 kg) when they were married. She was bright and pretty, and she was brought up in the Puritan tradition of order, strictness, and rigidity with daily prayers, church every Sunday, and Sunday school too. Martha grew up knowing that her mother was never to be bothered and her mother's position was never to be questioned. She was not even allowed to touch anything on her mother's dressing table. But Jenny, as Mrs. Graham was called, was not cut out to be a housewife and a mother. When Dr. Graham was away from home on house calls and rounds, Mrs. Graham was often left alone at home to care for Martha.

That problem was quickly and perfectly solved one day. While carrying Martha in her arms, Mrs. Graham heard a knock at the door. Standing there at the entrance to their home, luggage at her side, was Lizzie Prendergast, a former patient of Dr. Graham's.

Born in Ireland, Lizzie came to the United States to work as a maid. One day, she was brought to Western Pennsylvania Hospital. A pack of wild dogs had attacked her, and she was near death. Dr. Graham's treatment saved Lizzie's life. On that day, she vowed that when Dr. Graham was married and had a child, she would repay him.

Lizzie introduced herself to Mrs. Graham: "I am Lizzie. I have come to take care of the doctor and his family." Jenny Graham immediately handed the baby to Lizzie and said, "Here, take her." From that day until her death, "Sizzie," as Martha called her, remained with the Graham family as maid, friend, and companion. She was also kind of a spiritual leader who brought her Roman Catholic upbringing to this Presbyterian family. She was the dominating figure in the Graham household, and Martha remembered her as "not educated [but] wise . . . and utterly dedicated and devoted."

Lizzie loved the ceremonies of the Catholic tradition. To her, they had a theatrical quality.

When the Grahams were on a trip out West, Lizzie took Martha to a Roman Catholic church, and the memory remained with Martha for life. She remembered: "We walked into the building together as if entering a great hush, being let in on some important secret. I loved the lush, royal robes. I loved the formality, the ritual, the discipline. I loved the almost incomprehensible message which seemed to permeate the area." Though she didn't know it then, Martha was defining her life in dance, for all these aspects— formality, ritual, discipline—had the greatest influences on her work.

On May 15, 1896, just about two years after Martha's birth, her sister Mary was born. In March 1900, a second sister, named Georgia but called "Geordie," was born. And in 1906 when Martha was nearly twelve, the only male child, William Henry Graham, arrived. Her father really wanted a son and was very pleased. William's birth was a welcome event for the Beer side of the family too, because Jenny's two sisters also had daughters—six in all. At last, a son! Mrs. Graham pampered him and carried him around wherever she went. It got to the point that Dr. Graham once complained, "Why don't you put that child down and let him walk?" Perhaps all the pampering was an omen. When William was nearly twenty-one months old, he contracted the measles, which was very serious in those days. His condition worsened, and on January 24, 1908, William died of what seemed to be meningitis, an infection involving the brain and spinal cord.

Aside from this tragedy, life for the Graham girls was good, with Lizzie in control. They did as she said, and she in turn played with them and enriched their lives. "[We] had a large nursery with wooden blocks which we would build into cities, practical houses with windows, doors, and all those sorts of things," Martha remembered. This playroom was Martha's first theater. There they played make-believe, and Lizzie sang theater songs to them. Lizzie's love of theater struck a chord in Martha. One day, she invited Lizzie and her sisters to a performance in her room. When they entered, they discovered that Martha had redesigned the room as a theater, complete with a curtain made from a bedsheet.

Mrs. Graham was proud that her children had a theatrical flair and often made costumes and provided them with costume jewelry. She also enjoyed introducing them to theatrical experiences. During a trip to Atlantic City, the children were taken to see a Punch and Judy show, the most popular puppet show of the time. "When the curtain parted," Martha recalled, "there it was—another world, something to explore, delve into, make my own. There was a world created out of nothing. . . . It was a frontier for me in that I could enter it completely . . . a frontier of the imagination—perhaps the most difficult landscape to cross. I was spellbound."

LIFE IN CALIFORNIA

Soon after William's death, the Graham family moved to Santa Barbara, California. They had been to this beautiful Pacific coast town on one of their trips West and decided it would be a welcome change for everyone, especially for Mary, who was asthmatic and suffered most from the polluted Pittsburgh air. It would also be a change for the grieving Mrs. Graham. Santa Barbara was very different from Allegheny. It was a bright, clean town with small Spanish-style adobe homes on tidy streets that led to a sunlit beach. It offered a more relaxed way of life for the family, who would no longer have to wear veils and gloves to keep the soot away.

Jenny, Martha, Geordie, Mary, Lizzie, and grandmother Beer boarded the train and moved to the West. But Dr. Graham had commitments in Pittsburgh that required him to remain there for four more years. He visited his family several times a year. The train trip, which took nine days, was not very comfortable, mostly because of the heat and the dust of the dry land. However, Martha loved to go to the back of the train and look east at the life she was leaving and then go to the front and look west to her new life. "The train was taking us from our past, through the vehicle of the present, to our future." That trip became the inspiration for a dance she later created and called *Frontier*.

> "The train was taking us from our past, through the vehicle of the present, to our future."

Martha was overwhelmed by the changes Santa Barbara made in her life. Warm breezes tossed the window curtains around the sun-drenched rooms of their home. She could walk to the cliffs, look all the way down, and watch dolphins cut the surface of the Pacific Ocean. Her new friends and neighbors were Spanish and Asian as well as white Americans. Her neighbors included the Dreyfus family, who fled France after Alfred Dreyfus was falsely accused of treason at a notorious trial. Rather than remain in France, Dreyfus gave up his commission as a captain to become an American real estate agent. Martha, Mary, and Geordie played with the Dreyfus children, while their mothers became close friends and were active in Santa Barbara community affairs.

Mary and Geordie were turning into beautiful young girls. Mary had blond hair, blue eyes, and very long legs. Geordie had dark, curly hair and large brown eyes. But Martha was just 5 feet 3 inches (160 cm) tall and very thin, with a long face, deep-set eyes, and straight hair—in her words, "not what you would call an attractive child."

Though she had hated going to Sunday school in Allegheny because it was so boring, Martha began teaching Sunday school in Santa Barbara and found it just as boring. Boring too, ironically, were her Saturday-morning ballroom-dancing classes. In contrast, she loved her piano lessons and because she practiced often and hard and enjoyed doing it, she soon became a good pianist. Martha was happier than she had ever been.

CHANGES, FOR BETTER AND WORSE

In April 1911, during one of her father's visits, Martha and her family were walking down Main Street when Martha noticed a poster in a shop window. The poster advertised a dance concert featuring Ruth St. Denis at the Mason Opera House in Los Angeles. Martha pleaded with her mother and father to take her to see Ruth St. Denis. Martha's mother disliked Los Angeles and refused to go to the performance, but Dr. Graham consented. When the big night came, he pinned a violet corsage on his daughter's new gray dress, and they boarded a ferry for Los Angeles. No one could even guess what an important event in Martha Graham's life this turned out to be.

She recalled, "The curtain parted. The audience was still. Miss Ruth was doing a program that included her famous solos—*The Cobras, Radha,* and *Nautch.* Also on the program was her famous dance *Egypta.* I became so enamored of Ruth St. Denis as a performer; she was more than exotic—I realize now she was a goddess figure. I knew at that moment I was going to be a dancer."

Martha knew, but her parents were not so sure. Though Martha denied that her parents ever forbade her to become a dancer, we can be sure it was not a career choice they would have expected for their daughter.

However, Martha's secret desire was safe for at least two more years; she still had to finish high school. But a new Martha began to emerge. She paid special attention to her looks, to the way she carried herself, and to her effect on other people. One day, when her mother, her aunt, and her sisters were headed downtown to a carnival, they realized that Martha was not among them as they raced to catch the trolley. Her Aunt Re turned around to see Martha strolling along the street in her white dress, a bright red ribbon holding her newly created hairstyle in place. Martha noticed the conductor was impressed with her appearance, so she slowly stepped up onto the trolley car and sauntered to her seat like a swan floating in an emperor's pond. Aunt Re knew that "there was

Ruth St. Denis, seen here in Burmese Umbrella Dance, *had a powerful influence on Martha's career.*

something about her even then that made everyone stop and look."

That summer, Martha performed in an amateur production of *A Night in Japan* as one of thirty-seven geisha girls. For this seventeen-year-old, it was the chance of a lifetime to wear theatrical makeup and costumes and to perform in front of a real audience. When school resumed, she gave up her position on the basketball team to play the leading role in Virgil's *Dido, the Phoenician Queen*. Lizzie was so sure Martha was going to be a star that she once told Martha she would "be her maid backstage when [she] became a famous actress."

Martha's final high school performance was in *Prunella*, a play by Laurence Houseman and Granville Barker. Martha played the part of Privacy, the "timid yet loving aunt." *The Morning Press* of April 6, 1913, claimed: "The interpretation of Privacy . . . was a fine bit of acting. Miss Martha Graham's voice exactly suited the part and she was careful not to overact. . . . Sincerity and artistic appreciation of proportion marked every moment of Miss Graham's admirable work." They significance of Martha's participation in *Prunella* was that the play had interludes of barefoot dancing choreographed by Hope Weston, a graduate of Santa Barbara High School who was studying at the Cumnock School of Expression in

Los Angeles. Barefoot dancing became an important aspect of Martha's dance form.

Theater wasn't the only area that interested Martha in high school. She studied algebra, Latin, Spanish, music, history, and English. History was her best subject, but English was her favorite, especially when it came to writing. Her first contribution to the school yearbook—a short story called "Music and the Maid"—won third prize in a literary contest. She then contributed another short story, "Inez and the Wildflower," and became the yearbook's editor in chief. Martha also enjoyed sewing class and, to everyone's surprise, she was an excellent seamstress.

Slowly the pieces of Martha Graham's life puzzle were coming together: the influence of Lizzie's love of pageantry and Martha's enjoyment of open space, seeing Ruth St. Denis dance, performing in local plays, learning to dance barefoot, her creative ability, and her sense of theater all became important influences in her life.

The time had come for Martha and her parents to agree on what Martha would do after high school. Obviously, Martha wanted to perform on stage, and just as obviously, her parents wanted her to go to college, preferably Vassar or Wellesley, both well-respected women's colleges. But Martha held out for theater. A compromise was reached when she enrolled in the Cumnock School, a junior college that emphasized theater arts.

Unfortunately, after her first year, just when things looked their best, Martha's home life took a tragic turn. Dr. Graham died of a heart attack, and on August 11, 1914, he was buried in the Santa Barbara Cemetery. Suddenly everything "seemed as dark as Pittsburgh," to Martha and her sisters. Soon after, the family learned that their father's assets, a part-ownership in a ranch in northern California, had been sold and the money was embezzled. To earn extra income, Martha's mother was forced to sell their house, move to Los Angeles, and take in boarders.

CHAPTER TWO

FROM A DREAM TO A PROFESSION

Denishawn was a dance company named after its founders, Ruth St. Denis and Ted Shawn. St. Denis and Shawn also opened the Denishawn School, which offered classes in ballet, ethnic dance, dance history, and free-flowing movement exercises. In 1931, when St. Denis and Shawn separated, they dissolved the first recognized academic dance studio in America.

It had not been an easy time for them or for modern dance. At one point, a delegation of two hundred ministers and church elders marched on a city hall to protest "sacrilegious and blasphemous dancing" by the Denishawn dancers. However, progress was made. Their 1916 appearance at the Greek Theater at the University of California at Berkeley was the first performance by a company on that campus.

When Denishawn closed its doors, the company had produced sixteen years of American

*Members of the Denishawn company in 1916,
including Ted Shawn (far right) and Ruth St. Denis
(blonde in foreground)*

dance without the benefit of a single grant. They
had franchised Denishawn schools all over the
United States and introduced to the American
dance world three of its most important
founders: Doris Humphrey, Charles Weidman,
and Martha Graham.

A STUDENT AT DENISHAWN

Martha Graham was twenty-two when she applied to be a student at Denishawn and first stepped into the stucco building on St. Paul Street, about ten minutes from downtown Los Angeles. It was the summer of 1916, the second summer of Denishawn's existence and the last summer of Graham's enrollment at Cumnock. She waited for her interview with the goddess she had seen on stage five years earlier. Seated at a white piano was a heavyset man, who was smoking a cigar and reading a detective novel. He ignored her. Later Graham learned that the man was Louis Horst, recently hired as an accompanist by Denishawn and someone who would soon be an important figure in her life.

Miss Ruth, as Graham called her, entered the room in a flowing gown. She was blue-eyed and white-haired, tall, thin, and beautiful. She looked at Graham and said, "Dance for me." Graham replied, "I have never danced before and don't know anything about it." St. Denis then turned to Horst and asked him to play a waltz. Something overtook her, and Graham began to dance feverishly. When the music stopped, St. Denis was clearly not impressed. She thanked Graham and assigned her to Ted Shawn's class. She told Graham that she had "a great deal to learn" and that during her enrollment at Denishawn, she would study classical ballet and ethnic dances from countries such as Greece, India, and Egypt. In addition, she would be trained as a "thinking" dancer, one who could express emotions through the use of her body.

Graham's training with Ted Shawn included ballet fundamentals performed barefoot as well as character dancing and Western forms of Native American and Spanish dances. She also studied Oriental dance and yoga with St. Denis. She did exercises at the barre and other exercises on the floor. Graham enjoyed them all and was determined to make her body strong. Shawn understood Graham's limitations because he too began studying dance in his twenties. Starting at twenty-two was a rarity; most dancers begin their training as young children. But Shawn, a much better teacher than St. Denis, was patient and sympathetic. "From the first," he said, "Martha was conspicuous for her appetite for hard work." Martha also attended lectures about the history and philosophy of dance, seminars on Asian art, and classes in music, lighting, makeup, and other technical aspects of dance.

Unfortunately, Graham thought Shawn was "something of a dud." It was St. Denis she worshiped—the dancer who was sketched by August Rodin and sculpted by Gaston Lachaise, the noted

French artists; the dancer who was so graceful that she was examined by a team of German doctors to see if her body was the same as everyone else's; the dancer who admitted, "I was never a good teacher, but I can inspire like hell."

Graham would do anything for St. Denis. She took care of St. Denis's elderly mother when she came to visit; she washed St. Denis's hair; she posed for publicity pictures to advertise Denishawn and its concerts; and she taught dance to little children. But Graham did not fit the Denishawn image. She was not tall and blond and she did not have curly hair, so she was not permitted to perform. Often, in the middle of the night, Graham would go to St. Denis's studio. In total darkness, she created her own movements in order to be ready if St. Denis ever asked her to dance.

ON STAGE AT LAST

The opportunity finally came in the summer of 1917, but it didn't come from St. Denis. Ted Shawn had choreographed a solo Moorish gypsy dance—a combination of Spanish and Arabian movements—that he called *Serenata Morisca*. When he selected dancers to perform the work in concert, Shawn noticed that Graham, with her dark, brooding looks, would be perfect for the part, if only she knew how to dance it. When she told him she could, Shawn was surprised. "I got up quickly," she said, "hastily put on a skirt, and did *Serenata Morisca*." She had learned it by watching others do it. Shawn was impressed. "That is always how I wanted it to be performed. And you'll do it in San Diego," he told her. She did, and that day, according to Shawn, Martha Graham became a dancer.

In 1919, after Shawn returned from his stint in the armed forces, he made Graham his assistant, a position she held until 1921. Not only was she his assistant, but she was also his lead dancer. He choreographed a piece for her that had its roots in traditions of the Maya, Aztec, and Toltec peoples of Latin America. The dance, called *Xochitl* (pronounced *Zochil*), told the story of a beautiful maiden whose father creates an intoxicating wine from the flowers of the maguey plant. This father brings the wine to the Emperor Tepancaltzin, who becomes drunk from it and asks Xochitl to dance for him. He then tries to force himself on her, but she defends her chastity and eventually becomes his empress.

During one rehearsal, with Ruth St. Denis present, Shawn kept going over the same section, but he was not achieving what he wanted. Finally, Graham turned to him and said, "If perhaps you just told us what you want, we'll do it." It was the first time anyone had ever made a critical

Graham got great reviews for her performance in Xochitl, *1920.*

comment to Shawn. At that moment, St. Denis knew that Graham would be good for Shawn.

Xochitl was a lavish production in which many of the characters wore headdresses adorned with flowers and feathers. Moreover, it was the perfect role for Graham—a young woman who dances to rebuff the advances of a man for whom she had no respect. Graham could not have been more pleased. She had been given a chance to show how powerful and exciting she could be on stage.

During one performance, with Shawn partnering Graham, he lost his grip and dropped her. Having hit her head, Graham was unconscious for a few moments. But when she regained her composure, she promptly bit Shawn's arm, sending him racing about and dripping blood all over the stage. The scandal that followed created Graham's reputation for having a ferocious temper. Graham could feel how "a dance dominated her completely, until she lost sense of anything else."

Xochitl premiered in Long Beach, California, in June 1920. Then the vaudeville tour, produced by Alexander Pantages, went on to Tacoma, Washington, with Robert Graham, another Denishawn dancer replacing Shawn. *Xochitl*, composed by Homer Grunn, was a huge success and was acclaimed the first Native American ballet. The

Tacoma New Tribune called Martha Graham "a brilliant young dancer."

For the next two years, as the tour continued through the West and Southwest, the emperor, once danced by Shawn, was danced by a new dancer named Charles Weidman. Eventually, another Denishawn student, Martha's sister Geordie, joined the tour, which played as far north as Vancouver and as far east as Toronto. The strenuous schedule of three performances a day during the week and four on Saturday and Sunday gave Graham valuable experience, not only as a dancer but also as a director. To keep the company from getting stale, she would take out easy steps and put in more interesting ones. As her salary grew, she sent part of it to her mother to help with the bills and to pay for Lizzie. It wasn't until 1927, when Mrs. Graham married Homer N. Duffy, a wealthy businessman, that Martha felt she could stop sending money home.

During the 1921 tour, which finally brought them to New York City, Louis Horst and Graham developed a strong bond. Horst was an intellectual as well as a brilliant musician. He gave Graham books by the philosophers Schopenhauer and Nietzsche, and then they would sit on the cross-country train discussing the books for hours. Over the years, Graham was able to incorporate what

Louis Horst was a wonderful pianist and proved to be an important figure in Graham's life.

she had learned into her own lifestyle and even into her work. Horst was a rare find.

However, that rare find had a price. Horst was hired as Denishawn's temporary pianist primarily because his wife, Betty, was a member of the first summer class. Later, Horst became the company's musical arranger and orchestral conductor, transforming the concerts into huge musical extravaganzas. Over the next ten years, he also became an authority on dance and was able to offer criticism and suggestions during rehearsals. In fact, if he believed rehearsals were not going well, he would stop and insist that the dancers begin again, no matter how tired they were. He became indispensable to the company.

On the 1919 tour, Betty had developed tuberculosis and was forced to return to California. She stayed home with St. Denis while Louis went on tour, which provided income for both of them. Back in Los Angeles, St. Denis created a tour of her own, the Ruth St. Denis Concert Dancers, while Shawn headed for the East Coast. It was during this time that Graham and Horst became romantically involved. Because he was ten years older than Graham, Horst became a father figure for her. He put up with her temper tantrums, and he cheered her up when she was unhappy with her work. Sometimes he would scold her and force her to work when she wanted to give up. He criticized her when he thought she could do better, and sometimes he even slapped her.

Shawn's tour ended in New York's Apollo Theater. Graham loved being in New York. It was so different from her life in California. For her, New York was tough and intellectual—just the kind of atmosphere she liked. And this concert, which opened with a matinee on December 2, 1921, introduced her to the New York audience. Graham could not have been more pleased.

Ted Shawn's program consisted of twenty-one pieces, including several solos for Graham and the entire second act of *Xochitl*. Two piano solos by Horst were added to the program to allow time for costume changes. At their final engagement, Daniel Mayer, who represented such noted artists as Italian tenor Enrico Caruso and Russian ballerina Anna Pavlova, became Denishawn's new producer. Much to Graham's dismay, he brought back St. Denis to dance Graham's role, giving her top billing and a handsome fee. The company would tour the Southeast and then go to England, followed by cross-country U.S. tours, so that they could spread the Denishawn image. But for Graham, it was not so fortunate. Betty Horst, now in good health, returned to the company.

The London engagement was an unhappy one for Graham. With St. Denis dancing the lead roles, Graham was back in the chorus behind her and next to Betty Horst. Nevertheless, Graham was given an additional solo and a new dance, *The Princess and the Demon*, which she would perform with Charles Weidman on the Mayer tour. Graham continued to please the London press, but St. Denis's reviews were generally poor. Since Graham was afraid she would be dismissed if St. Denis saw Graham's good notices, she hid all the newspapers that praised her. But there was nothing Graham could do about St. Denis reading her own bad reviews. At night, Graham could hear St. Denis crying herself to sleep.

Graham continued with the company when it returned from England and crisscrossed the United States. The tour climaxed in 1923 at Town Hall in New York City with a twelve-performance run that included guest artist Doris Humphrey, who joined Denishawn soon after Graham. The New York critics considered Graham to be the only one in the company to dance with excitement or passion. These reviews, however, did not please St. Denis or Shawn, who still did not fully respect their young dancer.

MOVING ON

John Murray Anderson, producer of the renowned Greenwich Village Follies, attended one of Denishawn's New York performances. Afterward, he came to their studio and asked to see *every* dance Graham did. He then offered her a role in his next Follies. Graham, who continued to support her mother and Lizzie, knew that staying with Denishawn would not pay as much as going into Follies, so she reluctantly accepted Anderson's offer. Ted Shawn agreed to release her. Graham knew *Xochitl* was in good hands—the role of the maiden would now be danced by her sister Geordie.

As part of the Follies company, Graham performed exotic Oriental dances for Broadway audi-

Graham in the Greenwich Village Follies, a job she did not really enjoy, since she felt she was not creating art

ences. She quickly became a Broadway star, earning as much as $350 a week, which was a good paycheck for that time. Anderson produced *The Garden of Kama* for her—an elaborate ballet set in India and choreographed by Michio Ito, a Japanese dancer. Graham also danced *Serenata Morisca*, the piece originally created at Denishawn.

However, Graham really didn't enjoy being in the Follies. She had four solos each night, had her name in lights, and was paid a fine salary, but she felt she was not creating art. It was not where she wanted to be, and the showgirls made it clear that she did not fit in. Martha left the Follies in 1925. About this same time, Louis Horst left Denishawn and moved to Vienna to study composition. He returned just as Graham accepted a job at the Eastman School of Music in Rochester, New York, to teach music and drama students. Horst joined her there.

At first Graham was delighted to have an opportunity to direct her own dance department and to develop her own style of dancing with her own students. She began to experiment with various types of movement, rather than traditional ballet forms. She used basic movements such as running, jumping, and walking. Soon she created her own technique. But the experience was not totally satisfying. Though she had her own studio and as many students as she wanted, she explained that she was "troubled and restless" and wasn't "finding her own way as a dancer."

She was asked to choreograph shows for the Eastman Theater that were no different from the review material for Denishawn or the Greenwich Village Follies. After one year, she decided not to return. However, she had trained three students—Evelyn Sabin, Thelma Biracree, and Betty MacDonald. Evelyn Sabin, originally a student of ballet, knew as she studied with her that Graham was determined to create her own unique dance. Contraction and release were Graham innovations. She carefully examined how the body moved when it exhaled and inhaled. From this study, she was able to utilize contraction and release of energy. She believed inhaling empowered the body while exhaling released the spirit and the breath. It became the basis of the Graham technique. Another Graham innovation was fall and recovery. It was derived from moves that Doris Humphrey called "the falls." It relied on the time between the body being balanced and off-balanced, as when one takes a step forward.

After a year spent raising money and a $1,000 loan from Francis Steloff, owner of the Gotham Book Mart, Graham presented her technique in a fully staged concert on April 18, 1926, at the 48th Street Theater in New York City—the same theater as the Greenwich Village Follies, but there was no Follies show on Sunday nights. At that time in New York, it was against the law for dancers to perform on Sundays, so Graham's show was advertised as a "sacred concert." With Horst at the piano, she and the trio performed an evening of Denishawn-inspired works to a divided audience. Some people were confused about what they saw. Some hated what Graham did. One woman said, "This is simply dreadful. How long do you expect to keep this up?" Graham answered, "As long as I've got an audience." Others felt they had seen dance history in the making. Graham understood. "I'd rather an audience like me than dislike me, but I'd

"I'd rather an audience . . . dislike me than be apathetic, because that is the kiss of death."

rather they dislike me than be apathetic, because that is the kiss of death," she explained. More important, Martha Graham had found her niche. And she would no longer return to the Follies.

A few years before Horst went to Vienna, he had heard about Mary Wigman, a German dancer who was creating dances that did not rely on music. Wigman believed that the only thing necessary was some simple sound that complemented the drama in her dances. The idea impressed Horst, who had always believed that the dance must exist on its own, and the music was actually secondary. Then, in 1927, soon after he returned to the United States, he and Graham tried something completely new. Graham choreographed a piece called *Fragments* before Horst wrote the musical accompaniment. A precedent was set. From this point on, choreographers could create their own dynamics, and then composers would follow by writing music based on the dance rhythms. Once *Fragments* was created, Louis Horst devoted his full attention to Martha Graham as her collaborator.

Modern dance was gaining a reputation in the theatrical community. In that same year, *The New York Times* made John Martin its first dance critic and the *New York Herald Tribune* appointed Mary Watkins as its dance critic. Both Martin and Watkins championed the style of dance being developed by Graham and singled her out as their idol.

HER OWN STYLE

Until 1929, Graham was trying to find her own style while at the same time trying to shed the more romantic Denishawn style. Her dancers were well trained in the percussive technique she was creating. While ballet tried to defy gravity, Graham's dances were earthbound. And while ballet strove for beauty, Graham's dances were angled and bare. An example of her unique style was *Dance*, a solo piece. Rather that using her arms and legs in great swooping motions and rather than using the entire stage to create complicated patterns, Graham chose to remain on a small platform, clad in a red tubular costume. Using only that portion of her body between her shoulders and knees, she thrust herself angularly to the music's beat.

In *Heretic*, a dance she created in just one night to the music of a Breton folk song, a group of eleven women, wearing black jersey tube dresses, prevent Graham, dressed in white with her hair flowing, from penetrating the block they form. In essence, she was challenging the old traditions but was rebuffed each time she tried to break through. In *Lamentation*, she was a lone character experiencing the ultimate in despair, again in a tubular jersey, with only her hands, feet, and face showing. She was seated on a small platform, like a mummy, rocking from side to side, moving within the tube as if trying to break out of her own grief.

In these, as in so many of her other early works, she openly defied the rules of conventional ballet and deliberately shocked the audience with her power and starkness. She stripped dance of all its ornamental qualities, preferring to dance the miracle that is the human body. Classic ballet tends to convince its audience that what it sees on stage is basically simple. But Graham was eager to show a struggle because she believed that represented life. Though she had already gained some limited acclaim, many people misunderstood what she was trying to say. Some even accused her of mocking the art of dance.

In 1930, Graham restaged *Prelude to a Dance* as her contribution to the opening of the newly formed Dance Repertory Theater, a place for modern dance to present the individual and collective works of Martha Graham, Helen Tamiris, Doris Humphrey, and Charles Weidman. It was the perfect stage for these four dancer/choreographers, who wished to showcase their talents but who lacked the funds to produce a concert on their own.

Helen Tamiris began as a classically trained dancer and made her dance debut a year after Martha Graham made her solo appearance and a year before Doris Humphrey and Charles Weidman joined forces. Because she was not a Denishawn student, she brought her own distinctive style to dance, which she used in musical theater and in concert dance. She believed that dance must be dynamic as well as specific, spontaneous, free, human, and natural. Humphrey and Weidman became partners when they left Denishawn in 1928 because they felt St. Denis and Shawn were cheapening modern dance by participating in the Ziegfeld Follies, a vaudeville show much like the Greenwich Village Follies. After Humphrey made the accusation, Shawn defended himself by asking, "Do you mean to say that Jesus Christ was less great because he addressed the common people?" "No," Humphrey snapped, "but you're not Jesus Christ." "But I am," Shawn answered. "I'm the Jesus Christ of the dance." That remark did it. Shawn had gone too far, causing Humphrey and Weidman to leave.

This collaboration was daring because the four dancers were known only to a select audience who believed that modern dance was a new and blossoming art form. Most of the world didn't. Nevertheless, with Louis Horst as its musical director, Dance Repertory Theater premiered on January 5, 1930, at the Maxime Elliott's Theater in New York City. The four choreographers knew they were venturing into an important experiment. There would be no painted scenery, no elaborate costumes, no full orchestra playing, no story ballets. Graham, who was granted one of the five nights of production all to herself, thought that "a new vitality was possessing us. No art can live and pass untouched through such a vital period as we are now experiencing."

In his *New York Times* review, John Martin said: "Whatever ultimate judgments may be made as to the merits of the Dance Repertory Theater, the opening of its first annual subscription season . . . constitutes a date of the utmost importance in the history of American dancing. Never before have dancers of the first rank been able to see the necessity for sacrificing their own sense of independence in the interest of a common cause—in this case, the integration of modern dance in America." Unfortunately, for whatever reason—conflict of personalities, competition, or cost—the Dance Repertory Theater did not succeed, and the four dancers went their separate ways.

When she was not dancing, Graham was teaching and rehearsing with her group of dedicated young women at her 59th Street studio. Because she had no money to pay them, her dancers held daytime jobs. They left work early and gave up social engagements to be with Graham as she created new dances. They even came on weekends and holidays if she asked them. And though she was rigid and difficult, her dancers never questioned her. They were proud to be part of her troupe and understood when she told them, "My dancing . . . is the affirmation of life through movement." Much of her audience felt the same way. Some were there every time she appeared on a New York stage.

"My dancing . . . is the affirmation of life through movement."

It was in this same studio that Graham was invited by Leonide Massine to dance the role of the Chosen One in his production of Igor Stravinsky's *The Rite of Spring*, to be conducted by the famed maestro Leopold Stokowski on April 30, 1930. Massine, who was about the same age as Graham, was a famous Russian-born choreographer who worked extensively in Europe but was then preparing the U.S. premiere of the Stravinsky work. *The Rite of Spring (Le Sacre du Printemps)* is the story of a virgin who is chosen for her beauty to dance until her death, so when spring came the earth would be fertile. It was originally staged by the noted Russian choreographer Vaslav Nijinsky in Paris on May 29, 1913, and it created quite a stir. The audience was outraged by the music because of the score's changes in rhythms, tempos, and keys. Nor did they like Nijinsky's anti-ballet staging. Hissing, booing, and shouting filled the auditorium, and the ballet was withdrawn after several performances. However, some people hailed it as an avant-garde masterpiece. By 1920, when Massine staged it, popular opinion had changed, and it was accepted as an original work of genius.

It was not surprising that Graham and Massine did not agree on either interpretation or style. They were in such constant disagreement that Massine asked Graham to resign. But Stokowski wanted her to dance the part, so she swallowed her pride and agreed to do exactly as Massine directed. The production, which previewed in Philadelphia on April 11 and then played New York's Metropolitan Opera House, was a huge success. Graham knew that as a virtual unknown to traditional ballet audiences she had been honored to be in such an important production.

MAKING A NAME FOR HERSELF

That summer, Graham was the artist-in-residence at the Cornish School in Seattle, Washington. On the first day of class, she addressed the students: "I have something very exciting that I want to share with you. I have just come from dancing the role of the Chosen One in *Le Sacre du Printemps* on the great stage of the Metropolitan Opera House in New York City. I discovered something as I stood still for a long period of time . . . with the dancers all around me. I learned how to command the stage while standing absolutely still. And I'm going to teach you how to do that." She did that—and more.

On her way home after a very successful summer, she and Horst went on to Santa Fe, New Mexico, where they visited the strange, mysterious, and ancient religious sect, the Penitentes. Graham was intrigued by their ritual of walking through the mountains while whipping themselves with ropes. She was taken by the Native

Americans' bond with the land, their strong spiritual life, and their blending of native ritual with Spanish-Catholic ceremony.

Primitive Mysteries (and years later, *El Penitente*) was influenced by what Graham had seen and done in Santa Fe. *Primitive Mysteries* was introduced on February 2, 1931, to an audience that witnessed probably the most important work of Graham's career thus far. Unknown to the audience, however, that afternoon she had such strong doubts about the work's success that she nearly canceled its performance. Graham's three-part dance told the story of the Hispanic-Indian ceremony honoring the Virgin Mary, grieving at the crucifixion, and rejoicing at the resurrection. The steps were simple, the style unadorned, and the accompaniment by Louis Horst consisted only of flute, oboe, drums, and piano. When the curtain fell, the applause was deafening. After twenty-three curtain calls, Graham had clearly established herself as the center of modern dance. In her *New York Herald Tribune* review, Mary Watkins noted that *Primitive Mysteries* was "the most significant choreography which has yet to come out of America. . . . It is not only a masterpiece of construction but it achieves a mood which actually lifts both spectators and dancers to the rarefied height of spiritual ecstasy."

One year later, Graham's contributions to this new dance form earned her the first Guggen-

Graham (center) dancing in her masterpiece
Primitive Mysteries, *which was based on her*
impressions of Sante Fe

heim fellowship ever offered to a dancer or choreographer. She chose to use the $1,500 to study
with Louis Horst in Mexico.

When she returned to Greenwich Village, her
student enrollment continued to grow. She accepted students from all over the United States, but

this was the time of the Great Depression, and there was little money for Graham to pay the rent or for her students to pay her. The girls were not paid to perform either. If there was a profit at the box office, it went for advertising and theater rental. Her income came mostly from the daytime jobs she and Horst held at the Neighborhood Playhouse School of Theater and Sarah Lawrence College. The studio operated on devotion: the devotion of Graham to her goals, the devotion of Graham's students to her dreams, and the devotion of Horst to Graham.

Horst, who was now teaching courses in modern dance composition to the dancers, was always there for them. He gave them advice and encouragement, and sometimes he even gave them money. His influence was immeasurable. Graham would often become depressed. One night, Agnes de Mille, herself one of the great dancer/choreographers in the United States and a close friend of Graham's, found Horst comforting Graham in her studio. He claimed that Graham had rehearsed the girls and herself until they were exhausted because of all the changes she kept making. Graham, de Mille claimed, "worked them until midnight every night except Sundays and holidays, when she worked them all day." Horst scolded her: "You cannot work your girls this hard and then depress them. They will not be able to perform." He then told de Mille: "It's not worth it.

Every concert's the same. She's put us through the wringer. She destroys us." To that de Mille responded, "But Louis, she's a genius. Would you consider working with anyone else?" Horst answered, "That's the trouble. When you get down to it, there is no other dancer."

On December 27, 1932, Graham and her dancers were part of the premiere performance at Radio City Music Hall in New York. The opening of the 6,000-seat show palace included artists from the worlds of jazz, grand opera, ballet, theater, film, and even the circus. The Rockettes were there too. At first, Graham and her dancers were not accepted by the others in the gala production. It may have been because they looked and performed so strangely that no one wanted to go near them. To make matters worse, the audience did not like Graham's contribution. Though she was capturing a wider audience with each appearance, her style of dance still appealed to a limited number of people. Perhaps the audience would have appreciated something lighter than *Choric Dance for an Antique Greek Tragedy,* especially since it was the eighteenth act of the show. Graham's company was fired that night.

GAINING A REPUTATION

In 1934, the first modern-dance curriculum in the United States was launched at the two-year-old

Bennington College in southern Vermont. Graham, Doris Humphrey, Charles Weidman, and Hanya Holm were the main faculty, known as the Big Four. Hanya Holm, a student of Mary Wigman in Dresden, Germany, came to the United States with Wigman in 1931. She remained in the United States to open up a branch of the Wigman School, but she soon established herself in theater, film, and later television. She choreographed the original production of *My Fair Lady*.

Between 1934, when the program began, and 1941, when the School of Dance evolved into the School of the Arts, some of the most exciting, creative, and original choreography ever conceived was presented at Bennington. Two dances, *Panorama* in 1935 and *Horizons* in 1936, included scenic elements by the noted designer Alexander Calder. When the Bennington program was eliminated, only Graham, who had been its mainstay, was invited to return. She served as artist-in-residence until 1945.

Frontier, the dance that soon became Graham's most important work, was introduced in 1935. Its score was composed by Louis Horst, and its set was designed by Isamu Noguchi. Graham met Noguchi in 1929 when they were introduced by his half-sister Ailes Gilmore, then a student of Graham's at the Neighborhood Playhouse.

Frontier, 1935, was Graham's tribute to the American spirit. Its simple set was designed by Isamu Noguchi.

Noguchi was thrilled to have an opportunity to design for Graham because he knew, like his own work, her creations were symbolic rather than literal. His set was so simple: a rope from each corner of the front wall was pulled to the rear center of the stage where it met a small fence made of logs. Graham was very pleased and said, "Isamu brought me this very simple, elegant thing—just ropes individuating the distance, the trail and the tracks of the railroad train, and the inevitable fence that gets built as soon as the pioneers take over." He went on to design thirty-five more sets for her.

Frontier was Graham's solo homage to the American spirit. It was free, vibrant, and dynamic, ranging from small, muted movements to large, sprawling gestures. Her amazing use of space created the effect of her being part of the expanse of the Great Plains. She was also the model of the frontier woman, an example of strength and courage. Though it was only six and a half minutes long, the dance established Graham as a dancer whose inner core was distinctly American. *Frontier* acknowledged that she was truly the creator of American modern dance.

Toward the end of 1935, Graham was the only U.S. artist invited to bring her company to Berlin for the 1936 Olympic Games. At that time, Germany was led by Adolf Hitler, a Nazi who promoted discrimination against the Jewish people and others. Though she would have been paid handsomely and drawn international attention, she turned down the invitation, saying, "I would find it impossible to dance in Germany at the present time. So many artists whom I respect and admire have been persecuted, have been deprived of the right to work for ridiculous and unsatisfactory reasons, that I should consider it impossible to identify myself, by accepting this invitation, with the regime that has made such things possible. In addition, some of my concert group would not be welcomed in Germany. They are Jewish."

And though the Germans guaranteed them immunity, Graham refused to ask her dancers to go. The result was that no dance company represented the United States at the Berlin Olympics. Some time after World War II (1939–1945), Graham's name was found on a list of those "to be taken care of" if the Nazis had controlled the United States. However, when Graham finally danced in Berlin twenty-one years later, she danced *Judith*, the story of a Jewish heroine with a score by Jewish composer William Schuman.

Throughout the year, concert after concert posted standing-room-only signs. Audiences cheered and the press had only praise for the Graham Company. *New Theatre* magazine stated, "At the close of the dance season of 1935, Martha Graham stands almost unquestionably as the greatest dancer America has produced since Isadora Duncan, and as one of the outstanding exponents of the modern dance in the world."

Lincoln Kirstein founded a company called Ballet Caravan, which became Ballet Society and then became the New York City Ballet. He was not a great fan of the Graham technique—or, for that matter, of any other style being taught at Bennington—and much preferred traditional ballet. Nevertheless, Kirstein was invited to participate in the Bennington Session, and Ballet Caravan debuted on July 17, 1936. A young man named Erick Hawkins was in that company. Within two years, Hawkins had studied the Graham technique with one of Graham's students, had taken her class at her New York studio, and had convinced her to allow him to work for her. He became her dance partner in *American Document*, which traced U.S. history from the time of the Native Americans to the present day. It was the first time a male dancer had been part of her company and the first time she included spoken text in a production. The result was successful, and *American Document* went on to premiere in New York on August 6, 1938, and then became part of

Erick Hawkins (near center with Graham) was the first male dancer in her company, seen here in American Document, *1938.*

a cross-country tour. By then many more people were able to understand Graham's technique. Her audiences enjoyed examining U.S. history as seen through Graham's eyes.

Her good fortune continued as she welcomed Merce Cunningham into the company. Cunningham had studied as the Cornish School in Seattle and then joined the Bennington program in 1939 when it was housed at Mills College. Graham could now create dances that featured two male participants. Her first was *Every Soul Is a Circus*, a witty examination of relationships and the first

Merce Cunnigham (right), here in Letter to the World, *joined Graham's company in 1939.*

*Hawkins and Graham rehearsing in
Bennington, Vermont*

comic dance she ever choreographed. She was the
Empress of the Arena, Hawkins was the ringmas-
ter, and Cunningham was an acrobat.

Graham was so pleased to have men in her
company that she often allowed Hawkins and
Cunningham to conduct classes for her. Unfortunately, some of her students, feeling deprived of
her individual attention, left the company. Their
leaving was painful for Graham, but the company .
continued, and with the very theatrical *Every
Soul Is a Circus*, the period called "The Theater of
Martha Graham" began.

The New York World's Fair was officially opened on April 30, 1939. President Franklin D. Roosevelt delivered the dedication address, and Martha Graham and her company of twenty followed him. There, in front of 60,000 spectators, they danced *Tribute to Peace* to the music of Handel's "See, the Conquering Hero Comes" as it was sung by the Westminster Choir. *Dance Observer* magazine, a publication founded by Louis Horst in 1933, noted how ironic it was that dance was not an important enough art to be included in the World's Fair Music Hall Pavilion, but it was impressive enough to climax the entire opening ceremony. Nevertheless, the ceremony was televised by NBC. It was the first live broadcast of a dance event for the general public and a fitting tribute for Graham as she completed twenty-two years of professional dancing.

As the decade ended, Martha Graham's reputation had soared. Hers was now the foremost name in modern dance. She had learned to add humor, satire, and lightness to her dances without changing her distinctive style. As Graham lost her youthfulness and exuberance, she began to transfer those qualities to her dances. Her work then appealed to a wider audience and would continue to do so as the United States entered the television age.

GIVING EVERYTHING TO HER WORK

During the 1940s, Martha Graham created dances based on myths, biblical tales, legends, and other stories that focused on the human experience, and these pieces attracted greater attention. Some people tried to analyze Graham's work in terms of the personal experience she brought to the dance. Graham never allowed audiences into her private life, but many of the dances she created may indeed have been autobiographical. According to *Dance Magazine*, "She had a need to relive the destiny of . . . her heroines, she had to seek a complete identification with the female figure chosen." Graham left it to her audience to interpret what she danced on stage and to dig no farther.

Appalachian Spring, Letter to the World, and *Death and Entrances* may have captured moments of Graham's private life, though these moments were never made obvious to the audience. In addition, these dances featured men. This

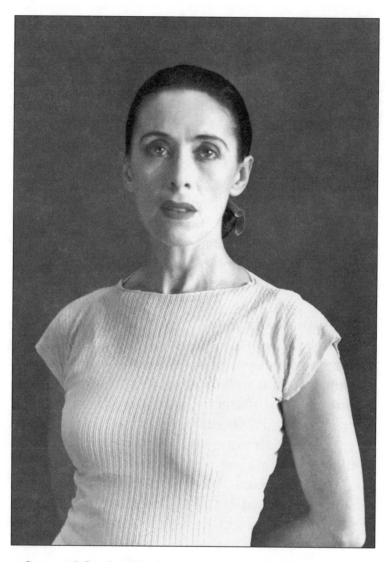

Some of Graham's choreography often depicted her troubled personal life, though the audience was seldom aware of the similarities.

▲ 67 ▲

was unusual for a modern dance group, since the performers were usually women. Male dancers were more likely to be found in a traditional ballet corps.

For Graham, the addition of Erick Hawkins and Merce Cunningham was the first opportunity for her to choreograph dances between men and women. This kind of dance was known in ballet terms as *pas de deux*, or steps for two. The opportunity to explore relationships between men and women and to include the male experience in her work was a great benefit. Of course, Graham added many more male dancers to her company, especially at the end of World War II, when returning veterans could receive free training through the GI Bill.

Erick Hawkins had a great influence on how the company was organized. In addition to teaching and dancing with the company, Hawkins took on the roles of manager and fund-raiser for the group. Certainly, Graham could have done these jobs, as she already had experience managing Denishawn's touring group. But Hawkins freed up Graham's time for more artistic pursuits. Besides, she liked Hawkins very much. Many in the company thought he was far too arrogant for a person who was not as talented as Graham and far from her equal intellectually. But for Graham's sake, he was tolerated.

Hawkins was thought not to be as talented as Graham, but she felt great personal attachment to him.

In the 1940s, the arts were not government-funded. It was up to the artist to get funds from whatever sources he or she could find. Hawkins had been successful in soliciting money from the Elizabeth Sprague Coolidge Foundation for two new works to be performed at the Library of Congress in Washington, D.C.

APPALACHIAN SPRING

It was at the Library of Congress that *Appalachian Spring* was introduced on October 30, 1944. The work was a tribute to the hardy men and women who settled in Pennsylvania, as Graham's forebears had. As part of the commission from Mrs. Coolidge, Graham was allowed to select composers of the music for her pieces. She selected Aaron Copland, the forty-four-year-old Brooklyn composer who created the scores for two "Westernized" American ballets: *Rodeo* and *Billy the Kid.*

Graham's unusual way of working with composers was derived from advice she received from Louis Horst. She presented a detailed scenario of what she wanted, based on her notes and quotes from passages she had read. She indicated where there would be an opportunity for a duet, solo, or a group dance, and then she left the composer to work it out. Graham didn't want composers to present a completed score before they understood what she wanted to accomplish. She hated cutting a composer's music to fit her dances.

Copland accepted the commission and composed a lush, glowing score based on a Shaker hymn called "Simple Gifts." This score won him a Pulitzer Prize in 1945, and he called it "Ballet for Martha." Some people detected a hidden meaning in that title since this ballet had to be done her

Graham and Hawkins in Appalachian Spring,
*a tribute to the men and women who settled
in Pennsylvania*

way and no other. Composers often found it challenging to work with Graham, since she believed that the choreography always led and the music followed. Perhaps Copland experienced some of this tension during the composing of *Appalachian Spring*, but rather than make his feelings known, he gave the score a title that showed who the "boss" was when working with Graham.

Basically, *Appalachian Spring* reveals the emotions of a young bride (danced by Graham, who was nearing the age of fifty) and her groom (danced by Erick Hawkins), as they take over a new house to become part of a new community. Other characters in the dance were the older woman, who was an adviser and protector, a frontier evangelist preacher (danced by Merce Cunningham), and a group of devout, young, unmarried women (danced by the company). The dance was exuberant and romantic, evoking a feeling of pride in the American pioneers. John Martin, *The New York Times* dance critic wrote, "Nothing Martha Graham has done has such deep joy about it." It was during this time in their lives that Graham and Hawkins fell in love.

Each of the characters had a solo that revealed his or her personality. For instance, the older woman represented wisdom, while the bride represented joy and anticipation. The groom portrayed the strength his family would need to survive, coupled with the warmth and assurance he gave them. The preacher represented religious authority when facing the unknown.

Appalachian Spring brought to Graham and her company an acclaim in the world of dance that they had not experienced before. But for all of Graham's newfound fame, she still maintained

Graham with Aaron Copland at a seventy-fifth birthday celebration for him in 1975

her privacy. She would not give interviews, and she would not pose for pictures outside the dance arena. Graham was in demand as a lecturer and guest speaker. In addition, she was invited to teach modern dance at the Juilliard School of Music, quite an honor for a dancer in a relatively new art form.

LETTER TO THE WORLD

Another dance Graham choreographed and performed was *Letter to the World*, which premiered at Bennington College in August 1940. In *Letter to the World*, based on the poetry of Emily Dickinson, we see evidence of how closely Graham related to Emily Dickinson, whose father was also a doctor treating people with mental illnesses.

However, Emily Dickinson was an American poet who gave up a "normal" life and, in her late twenties, became a recluse in order to find the truth. To Dickinson, love was something to be denied and to accept it was akin to committing a sin. Through her poetry, Dickinson sought out the truth, and this was the center of her life. Graham was like Dickinson in her focus on art—she was a dancer first, last, and always. And dance was the truth.

In *Letter to the World*, Graham created the role of the poet for two women: one who would

Graham in Letter to the World, *which was based on the life and poetry of Emily Dickinson*

speak and the other who would dance. At the performance in Bennington, Graham realized that the woman performing the role of the speaker could not dance. Though dancing was not a requirement for the role, a person who had no understanding of what dancers do would have a harder time keeping pace with them. Additionally, this speaker was presenting another problem. She was quite attractive and was diverting the audience's attention away from the dancers. When *Letter to the World* opened in New York a year later, Graham selected a dancer who could speak the part, as well as one who could sense the pace of the dancers and not upstage them as the first speaker had.

Erick Hawkins danced the part of the unattainable lover—the symbol of the world Emily Dickinson could never enter. And in the part of Dickinson's wit, which she often used to cover the pain she felt, Merce Cunningham danced. *The New York Times* called *Letter to the World* "a picture of Dickinson's mind." And for many in the audience, Graham was interchangeable with Dickinson.

DEATH AND ENTRANCES

In 1943, Graham premiered *Death and Entrances.* This dance was about the Brönte family, and again involved relationships that closely resembled Graham's own. Emily Brönte, who wrote *Wuthering Heights*, Charlotte Brönte, who wrote *Jane Eyre*, and Anne Brönte, who wrote *Tenant of Wildfell Hall*, lived in poverty with their brother in a parsonage in Yorkshire, England. In order to cope with a dreary life and a harsh father, the children began writing at an early age. In comparison, Graham had two sisters, and she had a brother who died very young. The Graham children had a strict upbringing, with their source of escape and entertainment limited to the plays and the costumes

"This work . . . speaks to anyone who has a family."

they created. But Graham said, "This work is not a mirror of my life, but speaks to anyone who has a family."

Graham prepared for this dance by reading as much as she could about the Bröntes. She took notes and then determined what kind of movements each sister would perform according to her personality. Graham wanted to shed light on how three young women were unable to free themselves from the hold of their father and ne'er-do-well brother and live according to their individual desires. She wanted to show how this affected them psychologically. During this time, Graham had been studying the works of Carl Jung, a Swiss psychologist who studied under Sigmund

Freud. Jung believed all human beings had a collective unconscious—memories going back to the earliest times, which could easily be identified because they were universal. Graham thought this dance could provide some understanding of how painful life must have been for the Bröntes and what sacrifices they made to write their novels. During rehearsals, she told her dancers that she wanted them to approach their parts as if they were actors. Erick Hawkins danced the role of the brother and also Heathcliff (the Dark Beloved) from the novel *Wuthering Heights*. Graham danced the role of Emily, the strongest Brönte.

Bethsabee de Rothschild, who was introduced to Graham by Hawkins, provided the $500 needed to create the score by Hunter Johnson. This marked the beginning of Rothschild's sponsorship of the Martha Graham Dance Company, which lasted more than twenty years.

BRINGING MYTHS TO THE DANCE

When Graham began to study Greek myths, legends, and biblical stories for inspiration, she focused on more intense human emotions, such as greed, jealousy, and self-hatred, which rarely had been expressed in dance before. Once again, Graham worked closely not only with composers but with set designers, using their work as an exten-

Cave of the Heart *used sets created by designer Isamu Noguchi.*

sion of the dance. Graham worked with Isamu Noguchi to create the sets for *Cave of the Heart*, which told the story of the Greek sorceress Medea.

Medea poisoned her rival and killed her two children because of the unfaithfulness of her husband, Jason. In this work, Graham danced the role of Medea, and Jason was danced by Hawkins. Noguchi created a headdress and gown as an extension of Medea's evil and jealousy. The headdress was a mass of coiled snakes, and the gown was designed of gold wire. Medea could not control the emotional outpouring of hatred and misery, which finally engulfs and destroys everything and everyone around her, including herself. This is symbolized by the gold wire gown, which eventually imprisons Medea.

Every one of Graham's dances, it seems, could in some way be connected to her private life. But more important was Graham's intellectual grasp of the human condition and how she could express it.

In *Errand into the Maze*, Graham used the legend of the Minotaur to show how hard it is for human beings to overcome fear. To Graham, the cave in which the Minotaur lived was a symbol of the unknown, and she called the Minotaur—a monster with the head of a bull and the body of a man—the Creature of Fear. The battle between the Creature of Fear and Ariadne, the person who enters the maze (danced by Graham) represented all the challenges a person must overcome in a lifetime.

GRAHAM IN LOVE

At some point, Graham began to realize that as much as her dances needed to be taken seriously, there was also a need to entertain an audience. She said, "I'm afraid I used to hit people over the head . . . in order to get them to hear what I was saying. Now I realize we don't have to be so somber . . . we must prove [that] our dances have color, warmth, and entertainment value." In the summer of 1948, at Bennington College, Graham created a dance that incorporated just those thoughts. The dance was called *Diversion of Angels*, and it concerned itself with the joys of being in love for the first time. It was also the first time Graham did not appear in the dance itself.

While production was being mounted, Louis Horst and Erick Hawkins had a fight. Graham, torn between Horst, her mentor, and Hawkins, the man she loved, sided with Hawkins. Because of this, Horst quit the Graham Company. Graham and Hawkins then left for Santa Fe, New Mexico, where they were married, to the shock and surprise of everyone. When Horst found out, it was said he grieved a great deal—despite the fact that he was still married to his wife, Betty, and also seeing Nina Fonoroff, a young dancer in Graham's company.

Perhaps Graham took *Letter to the World* to heart. Fearing the same fate as experienced by Emily Dickinson, she took the chance and, at age fifty-four, married Hawkins (though on the marriage license she gave her age as forty-six). But, even with the best of intentions, things did not go well for Hawkins and Graham. At one point, during a rehearsal with Hawkins and the group, she said, "One must give everything to [one's] work. Everything . . . even if it means losing a husband." Yet it wasn't as if Graham didn't make every attempt to help Erick. She choreographed at least two dances for him, but neither succeeded. She even allowed him to choreograph a dance for himself, called *Stephen Acrobat*, but that failed too. In fact, Hawkins's reviews were embarrassing both to himself and to Graham. The relationship became agonizing for Graham, and she had no close friends to whom she could confide her deepest fears. In one instance, during a dress rehearsal for *Death and Entrances*, Graham was nowhere to be found. This was unheard of, as all of Graham's dancers knew. Pearl Lang, one of her more prominent dancers, finally found Graham, alone and sobbing. Lang tried to convince Graham that Hawkins was not her equal, and Graham answered, "But I love him." It was as if Graham felt she was to blame for all of Hawkins's failures, and Hawkins used this concern to make Graham feel guilty.

For the American modern dance icon, the close of the 1940s was the best of times and, possibly, the worst of times. Graham was beginning to realize how close she was to becoming an artist who lives for her art—and for nothing else. She was hoping this wasn't true, for she wanted so much to share her successes with her husband.

CHAPTER FOUR

LOSS AND SUCCESS

The 1950s saw the beginning of the Cold War between the United States and the former Soviet Union. It was also a time when America was becoming more of a consumer society. After the sacrifices Americans made during World War II, and the concentration of U.S. industry on military supplies, this decade brought Americans a host of time-saving products for making life easier. There was more money to spend on entertainment, and the television set became the center of the average American home.

For Martha Graham, these changes had a positive effect. With more money being spent on entertainment, the likelihood was that more people would see her work. Additionally, since modern dance was truly a U.S. product, and Graham was the most well-known name in modern dance, the U.S. government asked her to perform all over the world as an ambassador of U.S. culture.

Bethsabee de Rothschild, of the famous French banking family, had always been a major contributor to the arts and sciences, with heavier emphasis on sciences. She also wrote and published *La Danse Artistique Aux U.S.A.,* a book in which Graham is mentioned many times. Once she met Graham and saw her work, Rothschild became part of the dance group and, finally, Graham's benefactor. Under Rothschild's patronage, Graham became a glamorous star. Graham, who never seemed to worry about how her group would be funded and what impression she would make on her audiences, began to see how important it was to look the part of the person she was—a symbol of American dance. For someone who always wore plain, stark clothing and gloves, Graham was transformed by Rothschild. First Rothschild paid all of the company's past and present debts. Then she made sure that Graham had all the finest clothing, jewelry, and accessories, to look the part of the star. And Graham enjoyed it. She liked to be seen riding around in limousines and going to parties with the rich and famous. She moved her school and her home to East 63rd Street, an upscale neighborhood in Manhattan, and changed the name of the school to The Martha Graham School of Contemporary Dance,

*Graham (second from right) enjoyed spending time
with the rich and famous, including (left to right)
Kathleen Turner, Madonna, and Halston.*

trying to avoid the modern dance term, which she
felt did not completely describe what she was
doing. And Graham continued to attract students
from all over the nation, including Betty Ford, the
wife of President Gerald Ford, and later on, the
singer Madonna.

TROUBLE FOR GRAHAM

Rothschild, along with other benefactors such as
actress Katherine Cornell and choreographer

Agnes de Mille, had underwritten Graham's first tour of Europe. But with all the wonderful things that were happening, Erick Hawkins still had to be considered, and he didn't want to be second to anyone, especially his wife.

When the company opened in Paris, Hawkins was featured. Unfortunately, Graham had injured her knees, and after the first night she could not perform. Without Graham dancing and with less than favorable reviews of Hawkins's performance, the company was forced to close. They moved on to England. There, Graham was in such pain that she couldn't perform at all on opening night. Hawkins did one dance and then left the company—and Martha—for good. The entire season was canceled.

Graham came back to the United States and left for New Mexico as soon as she could. Rothschild had promised Graham that as soon as she felt better Rothschild would fund another tour for her. In New Mexico, Graham found a doctor who did not recommend surgery to ease the pain of her knees, as other doctors had. Instead, this doctor said he would tell Graham what was torn and where it was torn, and he would leave it up to her to decide what the treatment should be. Graham agreed and decided to use weight exercises. She determined that when she could lift 25 pounds (11 kg) with her legs she would be healed. At the age of fifty-six, alone and in pain, feeling her age and a loss of self-esteem in her devotion to Erick

*Erick Hawkins left Graham—her company and
their marriage—during the company's 1950
European tour.*

Hawkins, it was amazing that Graham could put
all that aside and focus on healing her knees. At
heart, she was a dancer, and if she could not
dance, for her, life was over.

When Graham returned to New York, she was
still feeling the pain of her losses, but she was

determined to overcome her personal agony. With the fortitude of her Presbyterian upbringing, she exercised everyday, and everyday, she grew stronger. She consulted the person who first introduced her to Jungian psychology and learned how to ease her pain and stop drinking. Slowly, she came out of her torment.

BACK ON STAGE

In January 1951, Graham was back on stage in New York at Carnegie Hall, dancing *Judith*, a long solo, with music by William Schuman, set by Noguchi, and costume of her own making. The piece, commissioned by the Louisville (Kentucky) Orchestra, was a story about rage and revenge. It was based on the biblical story of Judith, a young patriot who lures Holoferness (an enemy of Israel) to her tent, wines and dines him, and then drives a nail through his head. Perhaps some would read Graham's rage at Hawkins into the dance, but if we look closer, we can see where Holoferness might have symbolized Graham's pain and agony, and Graham, as Judith, destroys it and goes on to further glory. In any event, no matter what people read into the symbols presented, it was a triumphant return for Martha Graham. The very elegant, well-bred audience at Carnegie Hall stood up and cheered. But at the end of the evening, John Butler, a close friend in the company, found Graham sobbing in her dressing room. There, on the table lay a book of love poems Hawkins had left for her, opened to their favorite and most intimate poem. While Hawkins could not live in Graham's shadow, he did not want her to forget him. She was indeed heartbroken. Graham and Hawkins separated in 1951 and were finally divorced in 1955. Graham still had the fortitude to overcome this emotional episode and, perhaps, use it in her art.

Graham continued to live in the style to which Rothschild had accustomed her. In her home, above her first- and second-floor dance school, Graham had a Japanese cook and a housekeeper. In public, she never used a cane, even though she still suffered pain in her legs. She never wore glasses, even though her eyesight was deteriorating. She never wanted audiences to see her suffer. That was a private emotion, and she kept it private. She certainly didn't want Erick Hawkins to see her suffer either.

DANCING THE WORLD

Against all the hidden troubles in her life, Graham the dancer was not hiding. In addition to her solo performance as Judith and also as Joan of Arc, Graham worked closely with the U.S. government to become an "ambassador" representing American art. In this role, she toured with her company in England, France, Belgium, Holland, Denmark, Italy, Switzerland, and Austria. The tour was a huge success.

Graham was an even greater hit on her Asian and Middle Eastern tour. In Indonesia, *The Times* reported, "This talented woman presented something of the United States we could wholeheartedly approve." One of the reasons for Graham's tremendous worldwide success was that her company was completely integrated. From the beginning, Graham selected members of her company without regard to race, and that had a profound effect when the company performed all over the world.

During this time, Graham was not without thoughts of Erick Hawkins. On January 19, 1952, Graham, along with John Butler and Bethsabee de Rothschild, attended Hawkins's first solo concert at Hunter College. It took all the control she had to see him backstage. And though he seemed to be more free in his movement, Hawkins still failed to produce dance works equal to Graham's.

Graham had to have new partners to replace Hawkins, and each new partner was compared to him. First, Graham was interested in José Limón, who was dancing with the Doris Humphrey Company. Limón believed that Graham would change his dance style, and he declined her offer. Then Graham decided she would have many partners. Among those who worked with her were John Butler, Stuart Hodes, Paul Taylor, Mark Ryder, Bertram Ross, and Robert Cohan.

All her partners were amazed at her ability to dance in her fifties and sixties, since by then most female dancers were retired. Paul Taylor, who later formed his own dance company, wrote, "Though the rest of us wilt with the heat, and sometimes drop with dysentery, [Martha] never misses a performance."

During Graham's 1954 tour of England, which didn't receive the best reviews, one person found himself overwhelmed by her performance. His name was Robin Howard. He was a very tall man, 6 feet 6 inches (198 cm), who lost both legs during World War II. He moved with the aid of crutches and artificial limbs. Howard must have seen something special on stage. In some way, Graham was able to transfer the movement of her body so that Howard could actually feel the depths of her emotions.

In fact, Robin Howard was so affected by Graham's ability to express emotions that when she returned for another world tour years later and England was not included on the schedule, Howard, along with the Earl of Harewood, paid for Graham and her company to perform at the

Edinburgh Festival. In the 1960s, when the company's finances were shaky, Howard paid all her debts, asking only that she accept British students. But when those students didn't want to come back to England, Howard opened The Place—the first modern dance school in Europe.

During her tours, Martha Graham had succeeded in gaining worldwide acclaim for American modern dance, and she was also being recognized in Europe as a choreographer. On tour, Graham met Carl Jung and his wife. And Graham finally met Mary Wigman, the creator of European modern dance. She welcomed Graham, praising her ability to continue to dance and choreograph. By all measures, Graham's touring years were a complete success.

When Graham returned to the United States in 1955, she learned that Louis Horst, her former mentor, had suffered a heart attack. She ran to his side, and they resumed their relationship. He moved closer to Graham's home on 63rd Street, where she could more easily take care of him as he recovered. To Louis Horst, Graham once again proved that he mattered to her.

Horst became well enough so that Graham could leave the United States on another worldwide tour in December 1955. Wherever she went, she was hailed. She toured Hong Kong, Japan, and China. She even went to Romania, then a

Louis Horst, seen here in 1938 with Hanya Holm, resumed his relationship with Graham in 1955.

country behind the Soviet Union's Iron Curtain. She said, "We must learn to respect our differences," long before anyone had ever heard of a "global community."

"We must learn to respect our differences."

CAPTURING MARTHA GRAHAM ON FILM

Aside from photographs, lectures, and Graham's notebooks, there was no record of her performances except in the memories of her dancers and audiences. Graham felt that the dance was meant only for that moment in time. She didn't want to be frozen on film. She was possessive of her technique, and she wanted no one to learn that technique except from her school and her teachers. And she also refused to allow her choreography to be used by any other dance company. In fact, she would not choreograph a dance requested by Ted Shawn because she felt he had neither the talent nor the imagination to perform the way she wanted her work danced.

In 1956, Nathan Kroll, an ardent fan of the Martha Graham Company, approached her about doing a film that would record her technique and some of her dances. At first, Graham was reluctant, even though the first two documentaries, *A Dancer's World* and *Appalachian Spring,* would be funded by Channel 13 in New York. Channel 13 was the prototype of the "arts" channel—programming of high artistic and intellectual merit and no advertising—and would eventually become the Public Broadcasting System (PBS) we watch today. The third dance, *Night Journey*, was funded by Bethsabee de Rothschild.

After watching how her dances were to be recorded, Graham became an enthusiastic fan of the filming. But, for some reason, probably having to do with her insistence on privacy, she would not speak before the camera. She felt people would be able to know what she was thinking, would be able to see her "insides," and this she would not tolerate. The problem was finally solved by having Martha sit in front of a dressing-room mirror and talk to the mirror, rather than to an audience. In addition, Rothschild donated an extra $10,000 to the effort and had a special dressing room built for Graham. The combination of solutions convinced Graham to complete the film, which was—and is—an excellent showcase for her.

She and Stuart Hodes danced *Appalachian Spring*. Bertram Ross and Graham danced *Night Journey*, and her company did various floor techniques and exercises for *A Dancer's World*. Though Graham's performance was less than perfect because she was in her sixties, it was still a marvel to watch the way her body moved. Graham liked the results so much that she allowed John Butler to film three of her dance pieces, in color, for *The Bell Telephone Hour*. Butler said he would film only if Graham promised she wouldn't drink. She agreed. And through the wonder of television, more people saw Martha Graham and her work in one hour than had seen her and her company on tour in one year.

Because she was so pleased with his efforts, Graham decided she would give John Butler a small birthday party the next day. But as Butler related the story, he told Graham he was so tired he wanted to sleep late, so he turned down her invitation. With that, Graham slapped him across the face and slammed the door of her dressing room. Graham always thought she was second to no one as a friend, and as a dancer.

WORKING WITH BALANCHINE

At the close of the 1950s, Graham received an invitation from George Balanchine, who, with Lincoln Kirstein, cofounded the New York City Ballet, to work on a project that would bring the world of classical ballet and the world of modern dance closer together. Graham was pleased to be recognized by the innovator of contemporary style ballet, which incorporated a more streamlined, athletic approach to the dance.

Balanchine and Graham collaborated on two works for both his ballet and her modern dance company. They were called *Episode I* and *Episode II*, with music composed by Anton von Webern, an Austrian composer.

Graham choreographed *Episode I*. She used her own company and four dancers from Balan-

*Three women of the stage (from left to right)—
Agnes de Mille, a dancer and choreographer in her
own right; Graham; and Mary Martin, an actress in
musical theater—at the opening performance of
Moscow's Moiseyev Dance Company at the
Metropolitan Opera House in 1958*

chine's company. The dance concerned two powerful and forceful women—Queen Elizabeth I,
danced by Sallie Wilson of the Balanchine company, and Mary, Queen of Scots, as danced by Graham. Their struggle with each other for power
was depicted by Graham as a tennis match, starting with the beheading of Mary, Queen of Scots,
and showing what led up to this scene. It was

unique, with lavish costumes and set design. *Episode I* again demonstrated the breadth of Graham's intellectual ability and her creativity. Furthermore, it was an early hint of what the women's liberation movement of the late 1960s was trying to prove in terms of strong, powerful women.

Episode II, created by Balanchine, was pure dance. The music was more abstract, and the dancers were not enacting a story. Members of Balanchine's company danced this part, with the exception of a five-minute solo by Paul Taylor of Graham's company. Graham received a standing ovation at the beginning of *Episode I*, but many in the audience thought Balanchine's work was far more contemporary. They didn't realize that Graham's was the more insightful of the two.

Graham and Balanchine did not work well together. Balanchine was just as renowned as Graham, and neither was interested in seeing the other's work succeed. In fact, at the close of the performance, neither Balanchine nor Lincoln Kirstein went backstage to congratulate her. While this venture allowed members of the dance community to recognize more clearly the relationship modern dance had to contemporary ballet, Graham would never work again with another choreographer or another company.

CHAPTER FIVE

A CULTURAL LEGACY

Between the 1960s and 1970s, Graham went through a period of triumphs and defeats. She was sixty-six years old when she choreographed *Acrobats of the Gods*, which debuted on April 27, 1960. It was her 141st dance. She considered this work a tribute to all dancers, whom she called "God's acrobats," but she also created the dance as a satire on the choreographer's art. Each time the chorus enters, seeking the help of a choreographer (danced by Graham), she hides behind a screen, designed by Noguchi, of course. The message was clear: the dancers were nothing without the choreographer's art. The music was composed by Carlos Surinach.

Phaedre, a dance performed in 1962 with music by Robert Storer, was the story of a young queen, her young lover, and her jealous older husband. There were many sexual overtones to this dance. In fact, the U.S. Congress denounced the dance as lewd. Of course, this drew to the performances audiences who had never seen Graham's work, more for the sexual content than for Graham's dancing technique.

Yet Graham had reached a plateau. While she was producing new dances as well as revivals, none of them were the landmarks that *Appalachian Spring* or *Letter to the World* were. She toured Europe and the Middle East from 1962 through 1967. In Israel, she helped Bethsabee de Rothschild establish that nation's first modern dance troupe, the Batsheva Dance Company, which would perform all of Graham's works. A similar school, the London Contemporary Dance Ensemble, was established in England.

GROWING OLDER

Graham received many honors and awards during this period, including the Capezio Dance award, many honorary university degrees, and the Handel Medallion, known as New York's highest cultural award. She was also recognized with a Martha Graham Day in Santa Barbara, California. In spite of these honors, there were events in Graham's personal life that were causing much stress. Doris Humphrey, her main rival in the modern dance world, died. Then her mother died. All of her benefactors from the Neighborhood

Graham presenting the Capezio Dance Award to
Ruth St. Denis in 1961. Graham herself received
this award soon after.

Playhouse were gone. And then on January 23, 1964, Louis Horst died. Her lighting designer, Jean Rosenthal, died in 1967. And her major supporter, Bethsabee de Rothschild, moved to Israel to devote all her time and most of her money to the Israeli dance company Graham helped create.

In addition, Graham's arthritis was increasingly troublesome. She had to wear her trademark gloves, whether she wanted to or not, because her hands were so distorted. She suffered with bouts of severe depression and began to rely heavily on alcohol to get her through some trying times. Her body was failing her.

Even though 1964 found Martha Graham to be the best-known dancer in the world's modern dance movement, things were not going well for her company. The costs of running the company were very high. Every craft was becoming unionized, from the dancers to the lighting technicians to the backstage workers. Graham's original dance group had not complained if they weren't paid—they felt it an honor just to dance with her—but her younger dancers felt differently.

As she got older, Graham had a great need to finish her work. Bethsabee de Rothschild continued to pay Graham's rent and to buy her gifts, but she could no longer afford to be Graham's only patron. Fortunately at that time, Ben Garbor and Bill Kennedy spoke to Graham about producing a film. Though nothing came of the film, these two men decided to support Graham's company. They made sure that Graham was dressed by the best designers, including Halston, who was then well known for the simple, yet elegant clothing he created. Graham was indulged as never before. She had her hair done by Kenneth, Jacqueline Kennedy's stylist. She had a face lift. Garbor and Kennedy wanted her to be a part of the "in" crowd, so they took her everywhere. At that time, discotheques such as Studio 54 were all the rage. People stood outside in line for hours, just hoping to get in. Graham made several visits there, where she was worshiped as an icon. Graham was even part of an advertising campaign by Blackgama Mink entitled, "What becomes a Legend most?" And surely no one could deny that Graham was a legend.

The problem was that Graham realized she had to give her dances to members of her dance group because she could no longer perform in them. She tried to hide her drinking problem, but her friends could no longer make excuses for her. Rothschild refused to provide further help because of Graham's problems with alcohol.

In spite of these problems, Graham continued dancing. At one point, while doing the famous death spiral in a revival of *Clytemnestra*, Graham could not get up from the floor as she usually did. Bertram Ross, her partner, improvised a step so that he could pick her up and then placed her against one of Noguchi's set sculptures to support her. Nathan Kroll, the man who had been responsible for Graham's *A Dancer's World* film, was in the audience. He ran backstage and pleaded

Preparing for a revival of Clytemnestra, *Graham was always the director.*

with Graham to stop dancing. She said, "I would die if I stopped. You all know that. The love I receive from the faceless audiences I cannot live without."

She began to use her dancers to move her, carry her, or support her so that she could go on. Clive

Barnes, who replaced John Martin as dance critic for *The New York Times*, advised Graham to leave the stage. Graham was furious, but she could not hide the truth from herself for long. When John Houseman was asked to take over the company for Graham, largely to preserve her work and keep the company together, she answered that if she could not dance, there was little reason to maintain the company. Houseman felt that Graham didn't care what happened to the company, and he gave up his directorship. The final blow came from Lila Acheson Wallace, of the *Reader's Digest* foundation, a major supporter of the Graham Company. It was reported to Graham that if she did not stop dancing, the foundation would no longer support her. Of course, the foundation still wanted to preserve her work, but to Graham the die had been cast. She would have to give up dancing or risk destroying what was left of her company and her contributions to the world of modern dance.

THE LAST DANCE

On May 25, 1968, Graham danced in *A Time of Snow*, a work based on Abélard and Héloïse, a priest and a nun in their old age. The dance revealed the anguish Graham was going through. The old lovers lie dead, while young dancers arise to embrace their bodies and place flowers on their burial stone. Graham was seventy-four years old, and many believed this was her farewell dance.

Shortly after she performed, she was admitted to the hospital and told she was dying. Though no terminal disease was diagnosed, it seemed that Graham's psychological problems were at work. Her world was crumbling, and her body would no longer provide for her. Her losses were drowned in a haze of liquor. She needed to remove herself from this world of self-destruction.

Between 1969 and 1972, Graham was hospitalized several times. Many from the dance world came to visit her, but according to Graham, it was Ron Protas, a lawyer and sometime photographer with no dance experience at all, who saved her life. Graham slowly recovered and went to Ben Garbor and Bill Kennedy's house to recuperate. In 1972, she collapsed again and was again taken to the hospital. It was at this time that Ron Protas stepped in and took over everything for her, from the school to the repertory company to Graham's daily schedule.

A SECOND CHANCE

Upon Graham's recovery, she was firmly convinced that she could start all over if she gave up her drinking, which she did. She wanted nothing more to do with her old friends. She believed she had a second chance with life, and this time she

*Graham (second from left) with (left to right)
Diane Keaton, Betty Ford, and Woody Allen
at the opening of* Lucifer *in 1975*

would run it the way she wanted, with Protas never far behind. She directed her dance company, she concentrated on choreography, and she had the notebooks of all her dances published. According to Agnes de Mille, the notebooks revealed a woman of tremendous intelligence. Graham had immersed herself in reading about all the subjects that interested her. She always looked for relationships among history, dance, and movement, and she used these relationships to create her dances. Graham was like the prover-

Graham and Rudolf Nureyev backstage after his
performance in Lucifer, *a dance she created for him*

bial phoenix rising from the ashes. Once she realized that being a dancer was not necessarily her
only reason for living, she could concentrate on
other aspects of the dance.

Graham was now eighty years old. Her company had performed on Broadway, and in 1974,
they completed a successful tour of Europe. In
1975, the Graham Company performed at the
Metropolitan Opera House, the place where tradi-

tion in all forms was the standard and where modern dance wasn't even recognized. But artistic excellence was recognized, and Graham's was the first modern dance group to be so acknowledged.

While Graham knew no one could replace her, she wanted to make sure people would continue coming to the company's performances. With that

Receiving the Presidential Medal of Freedom from President Gerald Ford in 1976

in mind, Graham decided that she would convince "stars" of the dance world to perform with her group. In 1975, Rudolf Nureyev, Russia's major ballet star, was coaxed into performing with the company. That June, she created the dance *Lucifer* for him. In 1978, she had Liza Minnelli, Judy Garland's daughter and a major star on Broadway, perform in *The Owl and the Pussycat*, with Carlos Surinach doing the music and Ming Cho Lee, one of the most famous Broadway set designers, creating the sets.

Graham was able to bring the most talented people in the creative arts to work with her company because she had repositioned herself as the legend that she was. Stars such as Nureyev and Dame Margot Fonteyn were just as honored to work with her as she was to work with them. And in 1976, Graham was the proud recipient of the Presidential Medal of Freedom, awarded by President Gerald Ford, who called her "a national treasure."

LIVING WITH ILLNESS

Nearing the age of eighty-eight, Graham proved that her star was once again rising, but it could not completely cancel out her health problems. In the spring of 1982, Graham was trying to finish choreographing a duet between two of her company's stars: Yuriko Kamura and Takako Asakawa.

She had problems with this duet and could find no solution that satisfied her. Pearl Lang, another member of her dance company, begged her to give up trying to find an ending for the piece. Graham had never given up before, but she now realized she had no other choice.

Within a day, Graham broke out in shingles, a painful rash commonly associated with older people and closely related to stress. Perhaps the illness was brought on by the loss of friends, the loss of her ability to dance, or her inability to find a solution to the closing of a dance duet. But the shingles were so painful that Graham often had to be carried on and off stage. At one point a nurse came to live with her and provide her with painkillers so she could get through each day. The public, however, had no idea of Graham's agony.

In a 1984 interview with Anna Kisselgoff in *The New York Times Magazine*, Graham described her daily schedule. She said she left the mornings open for doctors, dentists, or interviews. After lunch, she went to the school where she choreographed new works or rehearsed her dancers. At five o'clock, Graham went home, only to return later at night to the school where she continued to rehearse her dancers. She made no reference to her illnesses.

Another reason why the general public knew little about Graham's disabilities was because she was now big business. The Graham Foundation

Even as she grew ill and arthritic, Graham continued to work with her company every day.

received thousands—and sometimes millions—of dollars in grants. Because the rise and fall of the foundation rested solely on Graham, she had to appear healthy and able to take on whatever tasks were designated in the grants. By this time, the National Endowment for the Arts (NEA) had been created by the U.S. government, and the Graham Foundation relied on its funding to keep the Graham Company in operation. At one point, Graham was denied a $1 million grant, and she felt the NEA was attacking her personally. Ron Protas, who was now in charge of corporate donations to the Graham Foundation, was concerned that the loss of the NEA grant would hamper his effectiveness in soliciting funds from major corporations. But he need not have worried. Graham had recently won the coveted ribbon of a *Chevalier de la Legion d'Honneur* in France. He could counter any argument for denying corporate funds for the Graham Foundation with this very prestigious award that was seldom given to an American. Graham was hailed as a heroine worldwide. What company wouldn't want its name associated with this legend?

FINAL ACTS

In July 1984, Graham received a $250,000 grant from the NEA for the purpose of filming her company. In that same month, Graham held open auditions for dancers. Many potential candidates tried out, but even the few who were chosen had to accept intensive training the Martha Graham way. Once the new recruits met with her approval, they went on tour, with Graham making public relations appearances every chance she could. Graham at this time looked almost skeletal. She ate very little. It was as if she was obsessed with creating a complete legacy for others who would follow her, and the effort consumed her twenty-four hours a day.

By the fall of 1984, the Graham Company opened its season at the New York State Theatre with a new version of Stravinsky's *Rite of Spring*, which Graham created. It was underwritten entirely by fashion designer Halston. Terese Capucilli, a talented member of the company, danced the part of the Chosen Maiden. This dance involved intricate movements with special emphasis on the feet. It was meaningful to Graham because her father always complimented her on her own feet when she was a little girl. While the reviews were mixed, critics were once again amazed that this woman of ninety could create a dance of such technical achievement and emotion.

In the summer of 1985, Graham accepted a post on the National Council for the Arts, the governing body of the NEA. With Ron Protas, she triumphantly made the trip to Washington, D.C., where she was treated as a living legend, and she in turn provided sound advice to the council.

Back in New York, the school was running very well under the leadership of Linda Hodes and Linda Gray. Graham would often come to sit

*With First Lady Barbara Bush at a White House
tea held in honor of Graham*

in on classes. Additionally, Graham was very
much involved in the filming of all her repertory
and technique. Though Graham insisted that
achievements were more important than
archives, those archives were very important to
the financial health of the Graham Company.
They were created as a record of the company's
development and of Graham's technique. But they
also proved to be a good way to market the Graham Company and provided another source of
revenue. In fact, almost everything that could be

marketed was—including totebags, sweatshirts, and posters—all to fill the foundation's bank accounts. There was no question that the Martha Graham Company was operating as a business. For Graham, it really didn't matter as long as she could create and choreograph, and as long as she remained the most famous and most admired dancer in the world.

In 1987, Graham added three Russian ballet stars to her season. Maya Plisetskaya danced in *Incense*, and Rudolf Nureyev danced the role of the Preacher, with Mikhail Baryshnikov dancing the role of the husband in *Appalachian Spring*. Graham's role of the bride was danced by Terese Capucilli. While none of the dancers could take the place of the original cast, all were major stars and all added their own unique interpretations, which made the season most successful.

In 1990, Graham choreographed her last complete work, *Maple Leaf Rag*, with music by Scott Joplin. In 1991, she wrote her autobiography, *Blood Memory*. Some reviewers thought her book was not as accurate as it could have been, and some believed that she omitted major contributors and dancers who had an impact on her life. However, Graham was ninety-six when she wrote that book.

On April 1, 1991, Martha Graham died. She was in the middle of creating a dance, *The Eye of the Goddess*, commissioned by the Spanish

Mikhail Baryshnikov and Terese Capucilli
in Appalachian Spring, *1987*

government in celebration of the 500th anniver-
sary of Columbus's voyage to America. Her career
in dance spanned seventy years, and her legacy
continues. Like Columbus, Graham navigated
uncharted territories, alone and with every inten-
tion of arriving at a new destination that would be

unlike any in previous human experience. She redefined the concept of dance and its relationship to the body and mind. She spawned a new dance genre, one with greater sensitivity about expressing emotions. She defied traditional women's roles from the 1930s through the 1950s, and she became a role model for women from the 1960s until the day she died. Martha Graham was an artist through and through—an American original.

Martha Graham resting, just for a moment, from her life's work

CHRONOLOGY

1894	Martha Graham is born in Allegheny, Pennsylvania
1908	Moves to Santa Barbara with her family
1911	Sees Ruth St. Denis perform in Los Angeles
1913	Enrolls at the Cumnock School in Los Angeles
1916	Enrolls at the Denishawn School; meets Louis Horst
1919–1923	Tours with the Denishawn troupe
1923	Joins the Greenwich Village Follies
1926	Presents her first fully staged concert at New York's 48th Street Theater
1927	Opens her own studio in New York
1930	Restages *Prelude to a Dance* for the Dance Repertory Theater; dances the role of the Chosen One in Leonide Massine's *The Rite of Spring*; visits Santa Fe, New Mexico with Horst
1931	Creates *Primitive Mysteries*, a dance based on rituals she witnessed in Santa Fe, New Mexico

1932	Performs with her company at the opening of Radio City Music Hall
1934	Participates in the modern dance program at Bennington College; continues there for several summers
1935	Premieres *Frontier*, her homage to the American spirit; turns down an invitation to perform at the 1936 Olympic Games in Berlin
1938	Premieres *American Document*, tracing the history of America from the time of the Native Americans to the present day
1939	Performs in the opening ceremony at the New York World's Fair
1940	Premieres *A Letter to the World*, based on the poetry of Emily Dickinson
1940	Premieres *El Penitente*, a work based on southwestern culture
1943	Premieres *Death and Entrances*, a work derived from the lives of the Bröntes; accepts sponsorship from Bethsabee de Rothschild
1944	Premieres *Appalachian Spring*, a look at the American pioneering spirit, with music by Aaron Copland
1946	Premieres *Cave of the Heart*, based on the myth of Medea
1947	Premieres *Errand into the Maze*, an interpretation of the Minotaur legend
1948	Marries Erick Hawkins
1951	Is separated from Hawkins; premieres *Judith*, based on a biblical story, with music by William Schuman
1954	Meets Robin Howard

1955	Is officially divorced from Hawkins; cares for Horst following his heart attack
1956	Is approached by Nathan Kroll about filming her work
1960	Premieres *Acrobats of the Gods*, a tribute to all dancers
1962	Premieres *Phaedre*, a dance with many sexual overtones
1964	Suffers the loss of Horst upon his death
1968	Dances *A Time of Snow*, her last performance as a dancer
1969–1972	Is hospitalized several times
1974	Directs her company in a performance at the Metropolitan Opera House
1975	Creates *Lucifer* for Rudolf Nureyev
1976	Receives the Presidential Medal of Freedom
1985	Accepts a post on the National Council for the Arts
1987	Adds three Russian ballet stars to her company: Maya Plisetskaya, Rudolf Nureyev, and Mikhail Baryshnikov
1990	Choreographs her last complete work, *Maple Leaf Rag*, with music by Scott Joplin
1991	Writes her autobiography, *Blood Memory*; dies on April 1, in the midst of creating *The Eye of the Goddess*

A NOTE ON SOURCES

The primary sources for this biography were Martha Graham's own autobiography, *Blood Memory* (New York: Doubleday, 1991) and Ernestine Stodell's *Deep Song: The Dance Story of Martha Graham* (New York: Schirmer Books, 1984). Additional information came from the following works: Christy Adair's *Women and Dance* (New York: New York University Press, 1992); Jack Anderson's *Ballet & Modern Dance: A Concise History* (Princeton: Princeton Boom, 1977); Dore Ashton's *Noguchi East and West* (Berkeley: University of California Press, 1992); Daniel J. Boorstin's *The Creators* (New York: Random House, 1992); editor Jean Morrison Brown's *The Vision of Modern Dance* (Princeton: Princeton Book Company, 1979); Agnes de Mille's *Dance to the Piper* (Boston: Little, Brown, 1952) and *Martha: The Life and Work of Martha Graham* (New York: Random House, 1991); Howard Gardner's *Creating Minds* (New York: Basic Books, 1993); Trudy Garfunkel's *Letters to the World: The Life and Dances of Martha Graham* (Boston: Little, Brown, 1995); compiler Marian Horosko's *Martha Graham: The Evolution of Her Dance Theory and Training, 1926–1991* (Chicago: A Capella Books, 1991); Elizabeth Kendall's *Where She Danced* (Berkeley: University of California Press, 1979); Olga Maynard's *American Modern Dancers* (Boston: Little, Brown, 1965); Don McDonough's *The Complete Guide to Modern Dance* (Garden City, NY: Doubleday, 1976); Elinor Rogosin's *The Dance Makers: Conversations with American Choreographers* (New York: Walker, 1980); and Walter Terry's *Frontiers of Dance: The Life of Martha Graham* (New York: Cromwell, 1975). Also consulted were the following articles: Edna Ocko's "Martha Graham—Dances in Two Worlds," *New Theatre,* July 1935, p. 26; Tim Wengerd's "Martha's Men," *Dance Magazine,* July 1991; "World's Fair Opening," *Dance Observer,* Issue #9, May 1939.

FOR MORE INFORMATION

BOOKS

Freedman, Russell. *Martha Graham: A Dancer's Life.*
New York: Clarion Books, 1998.
Maze, Stephanie, and Catherine O'Neill Grace. *I Want
to Be . . . a Dancer.* New York: Harcourt Brace,
1997.
Pratt, Paula. *The Importance of Martha Graham.* San
Diego: Lucent Books, 1994.
Speaker-Yuan, Margaret. *Agnes de Mille.* New York:
Chelsea House, 1990.

INTERNET RESOURCES

Dance Links
http://www.dancer.com/dance-links
Provides links to dance-related topics, such as dance
companies and performance listings, dance schools,
and other resources.

The Isamu Noguchi Garden Museum
http://www.noguchi.org
Provides information about Noguchi's life and work, includes photos and links to famous people with whom he worked, and lists his most noted set designs.

Women in American History: Martha Graham
http://women.eb.com/women/articles/ Graham_Martha/html
Includes an article about Graham within the Women in American History site, sponsored by Encyclopaedia Britannica.

ABOUT THE AUTHORS

Gerald Newman and Eleanor Newman Layfield have written books for young readers on such diverse topics as allergies, drugs, racism, and writing college entrance essays. When not writing together or separately, Mr. Newman is a freelance graphic designer, and Ms. Layfield is an English teacher.

▲ 128 ▲